The Right Track

by Carmel Reilly

illustrated by Fatima Anaya

OXFORD
UNIVERSITY PRESS
AUSTRALIA & NEW ZEALAND

It was a sunny spring morning.

"It's a nice day," said Dad. "Why don't we go walking in the forest?"

"What a good idea," said Mum. "Let's get packing."

"What do we need to take?" asked Matt.

"We need to be well prepared," said Dad. "Even on the shortest walk."

"That means carrying food, jackets, jumpers and a map," said Mum.

Matt thought about this. Maybe it would be a good idea to take his new metal compass.

The family drove to the forest and parked in a nearby car park.

Matt looked around in amazement. "Those are the biggest trees ever!" he said.

"This is the biggest bag ever," said Petra, as she grabbed her pack.

"Don't forget that you can get lost out here," said Mum as they set off.

"So be careful to stick together, and keep to the track," added Dad.

The family followed the track through the forest.
They were surrounded by soaring trees, bushes,
ferns and vines.

Suddenly, Matt saw something blue float by. "Is that a butterfly?" he asked, following it behind a tree.

"Wait!" said Dad.

"It's all right," said Matt. "I'm still on the track."

They all watched the butterfly flit from one bush to another. At last it landed on a leaf.

Matt took a photo. "Lovely," he said, as the butterfly took off again, soaring high into the air.

Dad turned to the others. "Is anyone hungry?" he asked.

"I saw a picnic spot marked near here on the map," said Mum. "We could eat our lunch there."

The family walked on for a while. Then Mum looked at the map again.

"Oh goodness," she said. "I don't know if we are on the right track."

"You could check the maps on your phone," said Petra.

Mum touched the screen. "Useless! There is no reception here," she sighed.

"We are heading uphill," said Dad. "We might be able to see more when we get towards the top."

The family were halfway up the hill when it started raining.

"Pop on your jackets," said Mum.

Just then, Matt saw something up ahead. "Is that a cave?" he asked. "We could shelter there."

"I'm cold!" said Petra when they got inside.

"I'm hungry," said Matt.

"Luckily we are well prepared with jumpers and lots of food," said Dad.

Matt and Petra quickly put on their jumpers. Mum got out the food. Dad poured his home-made lemonade into metal picnic cups.

He winked at Petra. "Your pack will be a little lighter now," he said.

Soon the rain began to clear and the family walked back to the path.

"We need to work out our location," said Mum, looking out across the valley below.

"I can only see trees!" said Dad.

Matt asked to look at the map. "We learned about reading maps at school last year," he said. "I'm sure I will be able to work out where we are."

Matt took out his compass. "This way is north," he said.

"Is that the direction we should take?" asked Mum.

"Looking at the map will help us find out," Matt replied.

Petra stood beside Matt. "Look through those trees," she said. "You can see a hill, and straight across there is a creek and a building."

They all stared at the map, searching for the hill, the creek and the building.

"This is where we are," said Matt at last, jabbing at a spot on the map.

"Which means this track will take us back to the car park," said Mum.

The family made their way back slowly. They had to be careful as the path was slippery from the rain. Near the base of the hill, the track split in three directions.

"Goodness!" said Dad. "Which way now?"

Mum slowly searched the map. "I can only see one track on here."

Matt looked at his compass. "The one that goes towards the creek will take us back," he said.

The family walked on.

After a while, Mum's phone beeped. She held it up and touched the screen. "I can see our location now," she cried. "We are almost at the carpark."

Soon, they were back at their car.

"Not only did we have a good walk today," said Dad. "We learned some valuable lessons, as well."

"I learned more about map reading," said Mum.

"I learned it pays to be prepared," said Petra. "Even if it means a heavy pack."

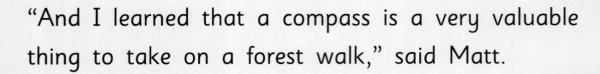

"And I learned that a compass is a very valuable thing to take on a forest walk," said Matt.